Marathon
Training Tips

A guide to successful marathon running.

Mike Stapenhurst - Deborah Prosser

Personal Logs Publishing

Acknowledgements:

Many thanks to everyone who participated in this book. Thanks also to our fellow runners in the Toronto Longboat Running club and the Fredericton Capital City Road Runners who have provided much valuable advice on running over the years.

Cover design: Christine Palmieri.
Marathon Cover Photo: Keith Stanley

Published by Personal Logs.com
Copyright © 2005 Personal Logs.com

ISBN: 0-9734241-3-3

First Edition 2005

Questions and comments about Marathon Training Tips should be sent to:

Personal Logs .com
64 Delaware Ave.
Toronto, Ontario, M6H 2T1
Canada

Email: feedback@personallogs.com
Website: www.personallogs.com

Preface

The goal of this handbook is simply to help you train for, and run, a successful marathon. Over the years I have run about 20 marathons with varying degrees of success. I've learned a lot from other runners and my own experiences about training and running the marathon during this time.

Debbie is a long time runner, but only recently started to participate in marathons. She brings a fresh perspective to the training tips that I'm sure you will find inspiring.

I have deliberately kept this book short so you can quickly read it and capture the key points. The aim is to provide you with:

> - Easy to read training advice
> - A quick reference to specific aspects of running the marathon
> - An overall guide to marathon training

I have tried to avoid repeating a lot of advice about running in general that you can find in the many excellent books and magazines that deal with the sport.

The focus here is on the marathon. I hope you will refer back to this book many times during your next marathon training.

Mike Stapenhurst

CONTENTS

1: Introduction 5

2: Picking a Training Program that's right for you 11

3: Getting Started 20

4: Performance Improvement 26

5: Staying Healthy 34

6: Recovering from an injury 41

7: Eat for success... 49

8: The Weekly Long Run 56

9: Keeping Focused 63

10: Pre-Race Week.. 68

11: Marathon Day Strategies 74

12: The Race... 81

13: Marathon Recovery 88

14. Last thoughts... 95

Appendix A: Pacing Chart 97

Appendix B: More Resources.......................... 98

Your Race Results 100

1: Introduction

"If you're in a hurry – slow down"! Chinese Proverb

Introduction

I have read a lot of books and articles on training for the marathon, but many of them are authored by 'elite' runners so I thought it would be helpful to give the average runner's viewpoint. I am still a competitive runner and like to participate in races and have won my age group on occasion. But often, just finishing with a good time knowing I ran the best I could, is enough satisfaction for me.

Another thing I have noticed is that training programs and advice tend to be generalized for everyone.

➔ I think every runner is different and what works for one person will not necessarily work for another.

Speed work is a good example; this is often touted as a must if you want to improve your times. I once had my best running year ever, and never did a lick of formal speedwork! I will take this into account in these articles, and will concentrate on underlying concepts as well as specific training pointers.

Some key topics we will cover in the book include:

> Finding the right training program
> Training strategies to build strength without wear and tear on the body
> Proper diet – finding the right balance to enhance your training
> Avoiding injuries – your main goal!

Thinking about it (26.2 miles??)

I remember the very first time I completed a 6 mile run, and I was feeling pretty good about it. Then I wondered how do people do this and then run 20 more miles all in one go? This was more miles than I was running in a week….

The answer of course is the same as for any sport – training and commitment, with commitment being the most important. As Yogi Berra was fond of saying "90% of this game is half mental"

The race itself presents some unique challenges.

It's the only running race I know that when you start, you don't know if you'll even finish!

What do you do if you "hit the wall"? (This is when you encounter a sudden drop in your energy level, your legs feel like lead and your will to continue evaporates, often around the 20 mile mark.) Should you walk…? Actually, on a hot day in Boston, Bill Rodgers once stopped, sat down, drank a Coke and then went on to win the race!!

➢ Halfway in the marathon comes at 20 miles!

So you want to run a marathon and join the hundreds of thousands of runners in North America who participate in this classic race event each year? I believe many runners who enjoy the sport look at completing a marathon as the ultimate challenge. Certainly, crossing the finish line is very satisfying, even if your body is complaining all over! Your first thought might be, I'm not doing that again. But by the next day you'll be thinking, if I'd only had a slightly better second half I would have been well under my goal.

Getting Started:
The first thing to do is select a race. Big or small? There are pros and cons for either choice. My first marathon was New York, and I reckon the crowd got me through the last eight miles – they were fantastic. Not to mention the other runners, who were always willing to chat and help the miles go by.
On the other hand I was up at 5:00 AM getting ready to catch the bus to the starting area. The wait before the race seemed forever. Then when we finally did start we walked! And I was on a schedule (this was my first marathon, remember)! So when we did pick up the pace I was weaving through the crowd trying to get back the time I'd lost. I probably ran 28 miles that day, the marathon plus the side to side distance as I tried to pass people. So a smaller (local) event can be easier from many points of view.

The next thing to do is tell everyone you know that you're going to run a marathon. That way it's harder to back out. Also if you can line up some folks to train with, this is a big plus.

Set your expectations.

My first marathon goals were totally unrealistic, given my lack of marathon experience. I crossed the finish line around the 3hrs 35minutes mark, and the person next to me said he'd been aiming for 3 hours. I was off my goal, and he was way off his!

In a later chapter we'll talk in depth about pacing and expected times. There are many formulae out there for predicting your finish times, based on previous results such as your 10K time. But if I were starting over, my goal would simply be to finish in a general time range, without a lot of pain and suffering. Your first marathon is a Personal Best (PB) time anyway.

The "Golden" Rule for beginning marathoners.

When you can complete the 26.2 miles comfortably, without hitting the wall or being forced to walk, and you can recover quickly in the days after the race, - then you have mastered the marathon distance.

Now you can think about setting time goals!

Debbie's Footnotes:

 Becoming a marathon runner is as much an adventure as it is a test in building personal stamina. When I started running it was back when the popular term was 'jogging'. Of course a lot has changed since then. I didn't stick to jogging long, but returned to running a few years later when Mike was training for a marathon. I wasn't very consistent at first, but as I continued my interest grew and I felt more capable. I began entering race events on occasion. These races made great milestones over the years and helped in making the decision to run a marathon. I've accomplished three marathons in five years, which is fine with me. Each time I trained for the marathon distance it was a challenge that brought a lot of fun and satisfaction.

We have run with running club members for many years. I found it helpful in listening to others experiences and strategies for achieving their particular goals. It's important to set realistic goals and have a few aids to give structure to the training program. Each time you choose to run a marathon the commitment to training must be there. Keeping motivated is important throughout the training weeks. In this book we hope to motivate our readers and help them achieve their goals in the marathon distance.

2: Picking a Training Program that's right for you

"Moderation in everything, including moderation!" - Oscar Wilde

Selecting a marathon training program that suits your abilities and goals is not as simple as it may seem. Each and every runner is different, with differing levels of experience and capabilities (just look at all of the different running styles you see out there). So how can choosing from only a handful of training schedules fit your specific needs? Let's take a closer look...

Abilities and Susceptibilities.

We're all good at some aspect of running. You have to be able to make a realistic assessment of your strengths and limitations. My own strength is the ability to run middle distances (Half marathon) at a fairly good pace (for me) and finish comfortably. My weaker runs are in short fast races like a 5K. I also find I am more injury prone doing this.

So, take a hard look at your previous race results, try and ascertain why you finished where you did, and set your marathon goals accordingly. *Know your weak points.*

The Training Goal.

Before you decide on a specific training schedule, it's worth looking at the *main goals* of any marathon training program. The reason for having a schedule at all is to provide a training structure for you to accomplish the following:

1. Build strength in the appropriate muscles
2. Build endurance – do any active sport (tennis, cycling, hiking) for 3 to 4 hours without much of a break and you'll be tired
3. Build mental stamina – when your body gets tired, it's your brain that keeps you going.

When you add all this up what you get is Experience! Your body will get used to the extra demands you place on it. George Sheehan used to call this *"miles in the bank"*!

The Training Schedule.

Now let's look at some training mileage charts. I've looked at quite a few marathon programs and I am astonished at the differences between them - from 9 to 21 weeks long, average miles per week varying from 30 to 50, speed workouts, number and frequency of long runs.... It's confusing!

So how do you choose your program?

1. Select your experience level

Some of the training schedules have different mileage charts depending on your experience and ability. Here is a typical classification chart:

➜ *These are only guidelines, and there is overlap between the categories. Many factors influence your ability to meet a marathon time goal.*

Category	Expected finish times	Number of Marathons	Other Factors
1: Beginner	Over 3h 30m	Less than 5	➢ **Your Age & Gender**
2: Intermediate	3h 10m to 4h 30m	More than 3	➢ **10 k results**
3: Experienced	2h 50m or more	More than 8	➢ **Previous injuries**
4: Elite	Competitive racer, sub 2h 30m marathon		➢ **Your personal goal**

2. Select the best training program for you

- Pick the category above that best fits your experience.
- *Be realistic* - the marathon is a tough race, so be conservative about your training goals (as well as your expected race pace and finish time)
- Look for a training schedule that applies to this level. If necessary, adapt the program to your own needs.

→ **Check with your doctor, especially first time marathoners!**

3. A good schedule will stick to sound basic principles:

- Incorporates the hard day/easy day approach on alternate days and weeks.
- Is not too long, (or short). I find a 14 to 18 week program to be the best, *depending on your current running level.* Beginner marathoners may need more.
- Is flexible. I firmly believe you should have the freedom to change your long run day, take an extra rest day, etc without compromising the overall results.
- Does not take you to too high a weekly mileage (Elite runners excepted!). About 45 - 55 miles should be the highest weekly mileage you will need. The beginner programs will be less.
- Has a gradual build up in your weekly long run distance. The long slow distance (LSD) run is the cornerstone of your marathon training, and you need to develop the ability to complete your long runs without over-taxing your body.

It's easy for beginner marathoners especially to get drawn into training programs that are really too ambitious for their level of experience. This is true even for those folks who can run fairly fast 10K races.

Things to avoid.
You may not agree with all of these, but they reflect my personal preferences and experience.

> ➢ **Long runs over 20 miles**. It's not necessary to run 24, or 25 mile training runs to have a good marathon.
>
> ➢ **Too many 20-mile runs.** One or two should be enough for most people.
>
> ➢ **Speedwork!** Again, I don't think you need to include this type of training for a marathon. It increases your risk of getting injured. If you run two or three races during your training period this will be sufficient.
>
> ➢ **Over-training**. Don't leave your marathon PB time on the training trails!

Training Schedules.
On the following pages are some training schedules I have put together based on research and my own marathon experience.

I have not included the elite category in these schedules. At the competitive level you should have a personalized schedule.

Feel free to adapt these programs to your own needs and abilities. I have followed combinations of levels 1 and 2 for my previous marathon training.

➜ You can download the Excel version of these training schedules from our website at:

www.personallogs.com/marathon_schedules

Schedule Level 1:

> ➢ Ideal for the beginner and occasional marathoner
> ➢ Has a relatively low weekly mileage
> ➢ Two rest days per week (You can do some cross training like cycling on one of these days.)

L = Long Run   R = Rest Day   T = Tempo Run   M = marathon Pace   E = Easy Pace

Week #	Sun		Mon		Tue		Wed		Thu		Fri		Sat		Total
1	6	L	-	R	5	E	4	T	3	M	-	R	4	E	22
2	7	L	-	R	5	E	4	T	4	M	-	R	5	E	25
3	8	L	-	R	5	E	5	T	3	M	-	R	4	E	25
4	9	L	-	R	5	E	5	T	4	M	-	R	5	E	28
5	10	L	-	R	4	E	5	T	3	M	-	R	4	E	26
6	10	L	-	R	4	E	5	T	4	M	-	R	4	E	27
7	11	L	-	R	5	E	6	M	3	T	-	R	5	E	30
8	12	L	-	R	4	E	6	M	4	T	-	R	4	E	30
9	12	L	-	R	5	E	5	M	4	T	-	R	5	E	31
10	13	L	-	R	5	E	7	M	5	T	-	R	5	E	35
11	14	L	-	R	4	E	7	M	4	T	-	R	4	E	33
12	15	L	-	R	5	E	5	T	5	M	-	R	5	E	35
13	15	L	-	R	5	E	8	M	4	T	-	R	5	E	37
14	14	L	-	R	4	E	8	T	5	M	-	R	4	E	35
15	17	L	-	R	4	E	5	T	4	M	-	R	4	E	34
16	16	L	-	R	5	E	8	M	5	T	-	R	5	E	39
17	20	L	-	R	4	E	5	T	6	M	-	R	4	E	39
18	12	L	-	R	4	E	8	M	5	T	-	R	4	E	33
19	10	L	-	R	3	E	6	T	5	M	-	R	3	E	27
20	5	E	-	R	5	R	-	R	-	R	-	R	3		13
Race	26.2		-	R	-	R	3	E	-	R	-	R	4	E	33

Total Training Miles: 637

➜ A tempo run is one where you run at a faster than normal pace for a good part of the total distance.

Schedule Level 2:

> ➢ This schedule calls for a little more intensity in your training
> ➢ Great for marathoners with some experience
> ➢ Has one to two rest days per week

L = Long Run   R = Rest Day   T = Tempo Run   M = marathon Pace   E = Easy Pace

Week #	Sun		Mon		Tue		Wed		Thu		Fri		Sat		Total
1	6	L	-	R	5	E	4	T	3	M	-	R	4	E	22
2	6	L	-	R	5	E	4	T	4	M	-	R	5	E	24
3	7	L	-	R	5	E	5	T	3	M	5	E	3	E	28
4	8	L	-	R	5	E	5	T	4	M	-	R	5	E	27
5	10	L	-	R	4	E	5	M	3	T	5	E	4	E	31
6	9	L	-	R	4	T	6	E	4	M	-	R	5	E	28
7	10	L	-	R	5	M	5	E	3	T	5	E	5	E	33
8	12	L	-	R	4	E	6	M	4	T	-	R	4	E	30
9	12	L	-	R	5	M	5	E	4	T	5	E	5	E	36
10	14	L	-	R	5	E	7	M	5	T	-	R	5	E	36
11	13	L	-	R	5	M	7	E	4	T	5	E	4	E	38
12	15	L	-	R	5	E	8	M	5	T	-	R	5	E	38
13	14	L	-	R	5	M	8	E	4	T	5	E	5	E	41
14	17	L	-	R	6	E	9	M	5	E	-	R	4	E	41
15	15	L	-	R	5	T	6	E	5	M	5	E	4	E	40
16	18	L	-	R	5	E	8	M	5	E	-	R	5	E	41
17	15	L	-	R	4	T	5	E	6	M	5	E	4	E	39
18	20	L	-	R	4	E	5	E	5	T	-	R	4	E	38
19	10	L	-	R	3	E	6	T	5	M	-	R	3	E	27
20	5	E	-	R	5	R	-	R	-	R	-	R	3		13
Race	26.2		-	R	-	R	3	E	-	R	-	R	4	E	33

Total Training Miles: 684

Schedule Level 3:

- ➢ You should have a good running base and marathon experience
- ➢ Great for the competitive runner
- ➢ Less frequent rest days per week

➢ *Remember, the harder you train the more injury prone you become!*

L = Long Run   R = Rest Day   T = Tempo Run   M = marathon Pace   E = Easy Pace

Week #	Sun	Mon	Tue	Wed	Thu	Fri	Sat	Total
1	7 L	- R	5 E	6 M	3 T	- R	4 E	25
2	7 L	- R	5 E	6 M	4 E	4 T	5 E	31
3	8 L	- R	5 E	5 T	3 M	5 E	3 E	29
4	10 L	- R	5 E	5 T	4 M	- R	5 E	29
5	10 L	- R	4 E	6 M	4 T	5 E	4 E	33
6	12 L	- R	4 T	6 M	4 M	4 E	5 E	35
7	10 L	- R	5 M	5 E	4 T	5 E	5 E	34
8	14 L	- R	4 E	6 M	4 T	4 E	4 E	36
9	12 L	- R	5 M	5 E	4 T	5 E	4 E	35
10	15 L	- R	5 E	7 M	5 T	- R	5 E	37
11	14 L	- R	5 M	7 E	4 T	5 E	4 E	39
12	17 L	- R	5 E	8 M	5 T	- R	5 E	40
13	15 L	- R	5 M	8 E	4 T	5 E	5 E	42
14	19 L	- R	6 E	9 M	5 E	- R	4 E	43
15	15 L	- R	5 T	9 E	5 M	5 E	4 E	43
16	17 L	- R	5 E	8 M	5 E	5 E	5 E	45
17	15 L	- R	5 T	7 E	6 M	5 E	4 E	42
18	20 L	- R	4 E	5 E	5 T	- R	4 E	38
19	10 L	- R	3 E	6 T	5 M	- R	3 E	27
20	5 E	- R	5 R	- R	- R	- R	3	13
Race	26.2	- R	- R	3 E	- R	- R	4 E	33

Total Training Miles: 729

Debbie's Footnotes:

 Choosing a training program can be complicated, especially for a first time marathoner. Being able to set realistic goals, finding information and answers to your questions, staying motivated during training are all factors in selecting a training schedule that will work for you. When you set this goal you'll look for the best event to fit your expectations, strengths, limitations and what you can learn from the experience. Our schedules will be most helpful when planning your weeks of training.

Training is a 'big part' of the marathon experience. You'll find plenty of advice and encouragement along the way. Joining a running club or having a buddy will be a sure way of keeping focused and motivated through training. What you bring to a marathon race is what you have achieved during training. We all learn from the experience and can be proud to be called a marathon runner.

3: Getting Started

"Eighty percent of success is showing up!" - Woody Allen

Like many difficult tasks, one of the hardest things is simply getting started. I always find the first few weeks of a marathon training program are difficult. Not because of the mileage, which is relatively low during this stage, but because of the discipline of actually having to stick to a program, day after day, week after week. When I'm not training for a marathon, if I don't feel like running, or the weather isn't good I can miss a day and it doesn't matter – as long as I'm not too far off my weekly mileage target.

The first 5 to 6 weeks of training are really an adjustment period, as you get used to following a regular running routine. The following tips should help you accommodate as you start your training program. I am assuming that you have already selected a marathon, and have a training schedule picked out with a weekly program and mileage goal.

Finding the time.
You need to find a time to do your running that fits in with all of your other daily commitments and activities. This isn't easy in the 'hustle and bustle' lives we lead today. Obviously, your running has to move up on the priority list and you will need to talk this over with your family!

The time of day you run is also affected by the weather. I lived at one time in central Illinois, with summer temperatures frequently in the humid ninety degree range, so running early in the morning was really the only option on some days.

Schedule your long runs.
Personally I prefer to do my weekly long run on a Saturday morning, but I know many people will choose a weekday evening like Wednesday. Pick

whatever works for you. However, it's always good to have a "fallback" day in case you miss your regular time.

Get a running buddy.

➜ Nothing will get you out of the door better than having to meet another runner. It also makes a nice change from the solitary runs, and certainly helps those long run miles go by.

Make sure though that your running partner runs at a similar pace to you.
When I was training for my first marathon by myself, my young son used to keep me company on his bike.

Running with a club?
In my earlier (& more foolish!) running days, our running club would go out on Wednesdays for a fairly hard 10 miles. We would all try and keep up with the front runners, even though their marathon times were 45 minutes faster than ours. This definitely did more harm than good both to our marathon training and our race times.

➜ Make sure you stick to your own pace goals when running with others...

Watch those aches & pains!
Depending on your pre-marathon training mileage level, you will be more susceptible to aches and pains due to the increasing mileage. Don't be afraid to take a couple of days off if you need extra recovery time.

➜ Don't run if you are hurting just to try and keep on schedule, as you are likely to end up injured.

I have devoted a whole section to avoiding injuries in a later chapter.

Check your shoes!

This may seem obvious, but your shoes should be in good condition. You'll be running 600 miles or more during your marathon training... I prefer to have two pairs on the go, so I can alternate them, especially during rainy weather.

Follow the program.

As you start out you'll be Gung Ho... resist the temptation to do too much at the beginning. Your goals in the first few weeks are to settle into a regular training routine, and start to increase your long run distance. It's best to increase your miles gradually as described in your training schedule. If you miss a day don't worry about catching up. There is plenty of flexibility in a 14 – 18 week program.

Keep motivated

I find that my motivation level varies a lot at the beginning for all kinds of reasons (health, stress, work commitments etc.). Reading running magazines or browsing the web for useful marathon articles helps me keep going. Running with others is also a great motivator.

Record your miles

Another obvious one. Make sure you record your daily mileage to compare with your training program. Not that you have to stick absolutely to your training plan (this is just a plan after all). But you should be following the general trend of increasing your weekly miles and long run distance as we talked about in the previous chapters.

If you don't have a running logbook you might want to get one for your marathon training.

Stick with it!
After several weeks of following your training schedule, you will adapt to the extra effort it takes to keep on track. It becomes part of your daily routine.

Debbie's Footnotes:

 When I started running it was about the time Nike introduced their famous motto 'Just Do It' and it was the message that helped get me out the door and has kept me running regularly ever since then. So once you've chosen a marathon, whether it's your first or fifteenth, this motto may help you to get started too.

Training for a marathon is a big commitment and you'll be faced with many options and challenges along the way. If it's your first marathon, or you've not run a marathon in a few years, it's best to give yourself plenty of training time. I'd suggest no less than 16 weeks and if possible choose a 20-week program. Starting out with a low to moderate weekly mileage and slowly building up will assure a solid base before getting into the long runs near the end of the training program. A longer period of training also allows more flexibility when something unexpected comes up. Like most people, during my past marathon training I've had to juggle between home, work, travel and vacation commitments. It's not always easy to work everything in and maintain the weekly mileage so if you are not fully committed you'll have difficulty in following through on your decision. Having a partner that also runs is a wonderful support and not only helps you accomplish your running goals, but is a great activity to share together. Most people are very accommodating when you let them know what your plans are and that you will be involved in training for a while. If you have non-running friends try and involve them in other ways, like meeting for an after run breakfast or lunch...they'll really appreciate the time you set aside with them.

 When training, it's always helpful to track your progress. I've always enjoyed journaling my activities and keeping a running log is a great way to keep you motivated between runs. It's also fun to look back and see where you've come from.

Most of all, stay focused on your goal and during those days when you're having a hard time to get started, remember the motto *'Just Do It'* and it will help keep you going.

4: Performance Improvement

"What the mind believes - the body achieves" - *Anonymous*

It's easy to get stuck at the same level of performance, especially in marathon training. In this chapter I want to talk about various things you can do to enhance your overall running capabilities. This doesn't just apply to marathon training - it will improve your running performance at any distance.

Key Factors

Here are nine key aspects of training that you need to consider during your marathon program

> 1. Weight Training
> 2. Stretching
> 3. Hill work
> 4. Cross training
> 5. Variety
> 6. Walking breaks.
> 7. The Inner Runner
> 8. Relaxation
> 9. Time Off

We'll take an in-depth look at each of these below.

Weight Training

I used to think hey, I'm a runner why do I need to do weight training, especially for the lower body? Well, running tends to strengthen a particular set of muscles resulting in a major imbalance in the muscular make-up of your legs. This can make you more susceptible to certain types of injury. Quadriceps especially can get neglected. For those of you who have already run a marathon you will know this is one of the hurting body parts after you finish.

→ You really need to be doing some weight training about three times a week (25 - 35 minutes per session is enough). I personally follow a full work-out routine to strengthen my arms, legs, lower back and abdomen.

Upper body workouts will also help to improve your running form.

Stretching.
Once again the experts differ on this; some say too much stretching can be a contributor to injuries, while others recommend stretching before and after a run. I prefer to do stretching and flexibility exercises after a run because I don't like the idea of stretching 'cold' muscles. Obviously you must not over-stretch to the point where you are forcing. After a long run it's easy to see how this could do damage.

➢ **You should include a moderate stretching routine at the end of every training run.**

You don't have to restrict your stretching exercises to your running time either. Yoga is a great way of improving the overall flexibility of your body.

Hill work.
We all like to run a 'flat' marathon course (Pike's Peak participants excepted!). So why run hills?

→ Hill training is a really good way to build up strength in those muscles that don't get so much of a workout on the flat.

This type of training will also improve your aerobic capacity as well. However there is a huge caveat to remember when doing your hill training. Do not force the pace or strain because this is one of the easiest ways to get injured, uphill or downhill. Where possible, I like to do hills in the middle of my run, when I am warmed up, but not too tired.

If there are no hills where you live, try the treadmill (elevated) or the stair climber machine at your local gym.

Cross train

I'm sure you've all heard this one before! But it definitely works, (if you have the time!). Swimming and biking are great alternatives, although too much  cycling can hurt you as well. I like swimming because it is a full body exercise that does not stress the bone structure. Running in the water (Aqua jogging) is another alternative.

However doing laps in a pool can get kind of boring. Cycling is a good exercise for using different leg muscles, and standing on the pedals to climb hills will definitely give those quadriceps a good workout. I usually like to get out at least once a week in summer for a 1 to 2 hour ride.

Mix it Up!

If I don't watch out, I often end up doing all of my runs at the same pace. I tend to start thinking about other things and my body goes into 'cruise control' mode. On long runs the only change is slowing down as I get into the later miles...! Depending on your marathon goal, I believe there is nothing basically wrong with always training at the same pace. It just doesn't prepare you so well for the actual race.

➔ If you are looking to improve your race time you need to vary the intensity of your training runs.

Sometimes I will run at different speeds during the same session, other times I will do the entire run at a faster than normal pace. These 'tempo' runs will enhance your aerobic capability and build strength. However - this is definitely a "listen to your body" process. If you decide to do a faster run, and find you are struggling right from the start, forget it! It is so easy to hurt yourself by over-stressing the body. You will also need more time to recover.

Remember the goal here is to train for the marathon, not a 10K!

Walking breaks.
Introduce walking breaks, especially on those longer runs. Since I hurt my hamstrings, I have used this technique to build stamina and endurance without the usual aches and pains. Simply put, walk briskly for several minutes (one to five) for every 15 to 20 (or more) minutes of running. You will be amazed at the results. Fewer next day aches and pains for one.

➔ Your marathon training goal is to be able to exercise continuously for 3 hours or more and walking breaks are a great way to accomplish this while reducing the strain on your body. Try it!

The Inner Runner
Much has been written about the 'Zen' of various sports, and the importance of the mental aspect in overall performance.

> ➢ Many successful elite runners talk about visualizing themselves crossing the finish line, and this helps them in the actual race.

I believe this can be a great help to marathoners if we can apply this technique to some of the key points in the race. For example imagine yourself at the 20 mile mark, tired but overcoming the feeling of 'hitting the wall'. This positive image will remain with you and help to get you through this critical stage on the actual race day.

Relax!

➔ In most sports you are going to perform better if you are relaxed, both mentally and physically.

Look at the lead pack of any major marathon – do they look like they are working as hard as they really are? No - they have settled into a steady relaxed pace, (albeit at 5 minutes per mile!). As you run, try to consciously relax your neck, arms, hands and legs. You will run much more smoothly and easily. In colder weather I notice my hands will tend to clench into fists, and I have to go through this relaxation process to loosen up.

Time Off
Professional athletes are very aware of feeling "burned out" mentally as much as physically. If you train all the time I guarantee this will happen to you... I know there are many people out there who run every day but I do not subscribe to that philosophy at all. Make sure you build "time off" into your schedule. This doesn't mean cross training either.

Sometimes taking 2 or 3 days away from your training program and from exercising in general can be a tremendous benefit.

You'll come back feeling refreshed and Gung Ho! But, <u>you have to plan for this</u> - otherwise you'll end up feeling guilty about missing your runs.

Count your 'day off' as a training day!

Debbie's Footnotes:

When your training gets a little too blasé...

It's important to vary your route and activities to avoid getting into a rut, especially if you're doing serious training. Like when you are doing more than one marathon a year. Two marathons within 6 months can put a strain on any running enthusiast. I found it difficult to stay motivated particularly a day or two after my long runs. As always, once I got going it was ok, but by varying my route and times of the day it was helpful just for the simple reason it's a change and I don't focus so much on how I feel, but more on the newness of my surroundings.

Another way to spice up your training is by adding some cross training activities. In summer I enjoy getting out for some rollerblading, biking and swimming as well as my training runs. The benefits of cross training can strengthen your muscles and add some needed variety to your schedule.

It's best to start your cross training activities early into your marathon training program. Your muscles will need time to strengthen with these extra workouts, so that you can still maintain the marathon distance on race day. Once you get up to those longer training runs of 16 to 20 miles, you probably will want to cut back on the cross-training though. At least until you start to taper off on your weekly miles again.

Adding some cross-training activities as well as changing your usual routes and running times is a great way to keep you motivated and interested when your training runs start to feel a little too repetitive.

5: Staying Healthy

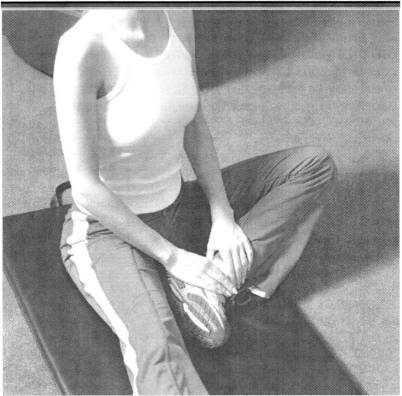

"I always loved running...it was something you could do by yourself, and under your own power..." - *Jesse Owens*[1]

---

[1] Famous pre-war sprinter. In the 1936 Berlin Olympics, he won four gold medals.

*If you've been consistently following your training program for a few weeks you should be feeling quite strong by now. This is when we need a red flag to pop up, with the words "**Slow Down**" written on it.*

Getting injured is the worst thing that can happen in the middle of your marathon training. An injury will not only impact your training, but if you try to "run through" it to stay on schedule (as I have foolishly done in the past), you could end up with a much more serious chronic problem.

➜ Moderation is the key to successful marathon training.

Although susceptibility to injury varies tremendously from one individual to another. Factors like age, diet, ability, and previous running experience all play a part.
So how do you avoid getting hurt? Here are some helpful hints.

Too much is too much!
Find the training balance that works for you. I have under-trained and over-trained for marathons, with poor results either way. Train too little and you'll have a hard injury-prone race. Train too much and you'll leave your best marathon time on the training roads because on race day your body will not be up to it.
If you are following a training schedule, but feel you are struggling to keep up, it's best to pull back, and modify your marathon goal if necessary.

Build your weekly mileage gradually

➜ Increasing your mileage too rapidly is one of the most common causes of injuries.

It seems so easy to add a few miles here and there to your runs to end up going from 20 miles one week to 30 miles the next. The rule of thumb is to keep the weekly increase to 10 - 15% or less of your previous week(s). I have gone from 20 to 25 miles in successive weeks without much problem, but as you get further into your marathon training you should stick to the guideline.

Alternate harder days with easy training ones. One of the 'golden rules' of training! This follows the principle of not doing too much at once. Your body needs more time to recover from long and/or faster runs. Your training schedule should be built around the hard day-easy day concept.

Shoes
Bio-mechanical problems are another major cause of running related injuries. The condition of your shoes plays a big part in this. If you run in "worn out" shoes you put more stress on problems like over-pronation.

➜ The guideline is to replace your shoes every 400 - 600 miles or so.

Heavier runners may want to change shoes more frequently. I normally have two pairs on the go, which is also useful when you have to run in wet weather.

Running Surface
This is another factor that can aggravate any skeletal issues with your legs and feet. Concrete is definitely the worst, so try and stay away from this kind of surface. Forest trails and woodchip paths are great for reducing the pounding on your legs, so whenever you get a chance to run off the road – take it!

Start slowly

Make sure you start your training runs slowly, before you get to your intended pace. This is especially true during marathon training when you are doing a lot of miles each week, without a whole lot of rest days. It is especially important to warm up gradually in cold weather.

Listen to your Brain?

The experts tell us "Listen to your body". This is great advice, but if you are feeling well trained and ready for any challenge I say "**Listen to your Brain**" as well and take things a little easier. Lay off the extra hard workouts or too many races during your marathon training period. I tend to be conservative and remind myself I'm training for the marathon, and that's more important than going all out in a 10k race too close to my marathon date.

Watch those aches and pains!

Pay attention to new aches that will come up as you increase your mileage. If you ignore these, they could become more serious, and prevent you from running altogether. It's better to take a couple of days off and recover, than to try and keep on schedule. Put an ice pack on any sore spots after your run. This helps the recovery and healing process. Running shorter distances on flat, softer surfaces also helps.

Feeling tired all the time?

Long training runs or too frequent training can weaken your immune system, making you more susceptible to catching colds and contributing to a general fatigue. If you see this happening you know you are trying to do too much. The remedy is to simply cut back, and even skip your long run that week.

Get enough sleep

You body re-generates itself during sleep, so you need to make sure you are getting your full quotient while you are training.

Do not cut back on your sleep to squeeze an extra hour into the day, as this will catch up to you as the time goes by.

Check your pulse

→ Your pulse rate is an excellent indicator of your overall condition.

Measure your resting pulse rate once or twice a week at the same time of day to establish your 'normal' rate. As you get in better shape, your pulse rate should decrease. Any increase over your normal rate could mean your body is fighting an infection.

Cross Train

As I mentioned previously, cross training and weight lifting help to counteract the imbalance in your muscular development that comes from doing only running. If you are cutting back on your mileage due to a minor injury, add a bike ride to your schedule.

Running with a cold

I know many people who continue their training if they catch a cold or 'flu. The danger is weakening your body further when it is already stressed by fighting the infection.

→ I definitely advise you not to try and do your long run if you have a bad cold or 'flu.

Keep Warm
On winter runs, make sure you have adequate protection against the cold and wind. Since your immune system may already be compromised by the training you are doing, it is very easy to catch a cold or flu' by adding further strain. I prefer to over-dress rather than the opposite on cold days. Take a hot bath or shower after the run to avoid getting chilled from your damp clothes.

Eat healthy!
Eating the right foods, and taking dietary supplements, can certainly help to keep you feeling better, and to ward off minor ailments. We have devoted a whole chapter to diet later on.

Debbie's Footnotes:

 Remember when you first decided to become a runner? You probably started out with the intention of becoming healthier, right?! No doubt this is still one of your underlying goals, except that the goals of winning at races and accomplishing more PB's has clouded this initial purpose.

Staying healthy is a wise and sometimes difficult thing to do as you set more and more expectations on to your running goals. However, if you stay on top of your information on diet, nutrition and how to recover from hard workouts, it is possible to stay healthy and injury free too.

So what about diets/nutrition (general lifestyle) and recovery information? There is just so much information out there; it's difficult to filter out what is right for you.

Following hard training workouts the recovery process is very important. Most of the advice I've gleaned focuses on nutrition and rest. I've noticed that I'm slower recovering from races and long runs than I used to be five or six years ago. Although my diet has remained much the same, I've kept a running log each year and noticed that I'm not taking as many easy runs or rest days off before and after hard workout runs. All in all, you have to do your own analysis of what is affecting your training and recovery times.

6: Recovering from an injury

"Eventually you learn that the competition is against the little voice inside you that wants you to quit." -George Sheehan[2]

---

[2] George Sheehan was a well-respected 'running philosopher' of the 1970's. Learn more about him at www.georgesheehan.com

So the worst has happened and you get injured or sick. You're right on schedule with your training so far and you don't want to miss out on too many training runs. What do you do?

First, assess the damage:

The severity of your injury can be categorized as follows:

Level 1: You only feel pain in the injured area when you are running. Walking is OK.

Level 2: You feel discomfort when walking as well as running, or when moving your muscles in a certain range of motion.

Level 3: The injured area hurts continuously.

Treatment

Level 1 can easily become level 2 if you continue running as before. You can try self treatment for a few days and look for improvement. If this isn't happening you should see your physician.

Level 2 injuries will probably require a visit to your doctor, although you can try waiting for a day or so to see if there is any improvement.

Level 3 – you should consult your physician right away because this type of injury can easily become worse if not treated appropriately.

Generally you will want to go through a recovery phase to get rid of the pain, and then move into a maintenance phase to build back muscle strength and endurance.

Quick Fixes

Ice is a great remedy for muscular pains and sore joints. An ice pack over the injured part for 10 to 15 minutes two or three times a day will help speed up the healing process.

Anti-inflammatory agents like Ibuprofen can also help a lot in your recovery. I often take an aspirin before going to bed after my weekly long run day. I find this helps me sleep better. Like any drug though, be prudent about your consumption level.

Try 'RICE'

RICE stands for:

> - Rest
> - Ice
> - Compression
> - Elevation

This is a popular remedy you can try for simple problems.

> - Rest - take time off to allow the muscle tissue to repair itself.
> - Use ice as mentioned above.
> - Compression, such as using an elastic bandage, can help support the injured area.
> - Finally, elevating the leg to promote blood circulation can also help speed up recovery.

Common Injuries

Most running injuries are caused either by training errors (usually over-training) or by biomechanical problems such as over-pronation. Quite often an injury will appear almost instantly, although it may have been due to a gradual weakening of the muscle area over time.

Following are some of the more common running-related injuries. Consult your sports medicine doctor if any of these persist or re-occur.

Shin Splints:
Soreness along the front of the shins. Can be caused by hard runs, over-pronation and muscular imbalance. Use ice after your runs; make sure to stretch the calf muscles and lower leg.

Achilles Tendonitis:
This is pain at the rear of your ankle. Often caused by too much training, poor heel support (worn out shoes or excessive pronation) or a lot of speed work. You need to take some time off and rest. Ice will help. Make sure to stretch properly and resume running slowly.

Plantar Fascilitis:
Pain beginning at the base of your heel. Can be caused by a lack of arch support or by over-training. Make sure your shoes are in good condition, with proper arch support. Ice the area, and reduce your running. Take some Ibuprofen to help reduce the swelling,

Knee Pain:
This is one of the most common problems facing runners. Causes include worn shoes, over-use and prior weakness from other sports like football or tennis. The knee is a problem area and can be hard to rehabilitate. Rest, ice, and appropriate stretching are called for. It's best to proceed slowly through the recovery phase, because this is an injury that can re-occur easily.

Sore Hamstring:
This is often caused by over-use or a lot of hill work. Hamstring pain can become chronic if you do not take care. Time off and cross training activities like swimming can help. I have used an elastic bandage for support when I am sitting at my desk or driving, and found this helps.

Alternate exercises
If you're like me you don't like being out of action on the injured list, especially when you are trying to train for a marathon! An excellent way to help maintain your fitness level while you are injured and unable to run, is to do an alternative sport (with the approval of your physician as appropriate!) Consider using the following alternatives when you are unable to run.

> ➢ **Swimming** and/or aqua-jogging is a great way to keep up your aerobic training and re-habilitate injured muscles and tendons. This is a resistance-free exercise that is very easy on the body.

> ➢ **Walking** is also excellent as long as you are not putting stress on the injury. This is also a good way of gradually easing back into your running. You can start by walking for say 15 minutes and then do 5 minutes running. As you progress this will reverse to 15 running and 5 walking, and then gradually reduce the walking breaks. I have integrated walking breaks into my regular running, because I believe it gives your body a chance to recover even during the exercise period.
>
> ➢ **Cycling** is another option, but you really need to be careful and not put strain on the injured part. Hills can be especially strenuous on a bike.

Post-recovery

Have you ever recovered from an injury, and resumed your running only to have the injury re-surface. This is the most frustrating thing that can happen during your training (or any time for that matter!). There are some things you can do to avoid this situation:

➢ Give it some extra time. Even though the injured area feels fine, it is probably still in the recuperation phase and very susceptible to stress.

➢ Run at a slower pace for about a week. Not only will this reduce the strain, it exercises the companion muscles that support the injured area.

➢ Try walking during your runs.

➢ Avoid races and speedwork for three weeks or more. Depending on the severity of your injury you might want to eliminate any hard runs before the marathon.

→ Remember - age is also a big factor. The older you get, the longer your body needs time to heal.

Colds and 'Flu

If you do catch a cold, you have to be careful not to make things worse by continuing to train at your normal level. Don't add stress to your body by trying to do your long run if you have a bad cold or 'flu. If I catch a cold during my marathon training I take a lot more care of myself (e.g. a day off work) than I normally would.

The best recipe for a cold is well known - rest, drink a lot of fluids, and take aspirin or similar medication. Although you might feel miserable, just remember it's usually easier to recover from a cold than from a running injury!

Debbie's Footnotes:

 Ever been a member of a running club? Well then, you know that for most people, being a runner will eventually lead to some kind of injury. (Now don't let that stop you from joining a club!) Members will share their experiences with others and lots of lessons on injury prevention can be learned the easy way…. from someone else's recovery.

So, what if you still get injured? Most articles I've read will advise you to back off from your training as soon as you begin to feel an injury coming on. This could be a feeling of strain and tiredness, or soreness and even pain in some area of the body. These are all signs of a possible injury.

Many runners will start to use the icing method for strain or soreness and this is often all it takes along with a few lighter days to provide the rest and recovery needed to prevent an injury. Most of the time, lighter days, icing, a couple of aspirin and going to bed early will help you to get back on the road and keep you running. Here's hoping you never have to recover from a serious injury from running or training.

Over/under training combined with over exertion will often lead to injury especially during or after race events. These would make up the bulk of the injured runners I've known over the years. I had to abandon my first marathon training over half way through because of shin splints from increasing my miles and intensity too quickly. My shins were so bad that I couldn't run for several weeks without pain. I'm very careful in training now and have not suffered from a serious shin problem since. When a marathon-training program is added to your running experience it won't take long to learn where your weaknesses lie. I think most people have some indication of where they're likely to get injured before it actually happens.

Wearing improper shoes is also a common way to get injured. Don't wear your shoes until the soles wear out. When shoes have around 400 to 600 miles of wear throw them out or give them to a needy cause. They may still look OK, but they are worn out for any continued training miles. Also, it's important to get the right type of shoe for your running style. I've found that running store staff is very good at advising on what type of shoe you require. Just be careful to get a few different opinions as stores will only carry certain brands and you'll need to try different stores before choosing a shoe that is good for you.

7: Eat for success

"If you feel like eating, eat. Let your body tell you what it wants." - Joan Benoit Samuelson[3]

---

[3] 1984 Olympic Marathon Champion

Many of us who have been running for a number of years probably recall that diet consideration didn't play a big part in our training program. We used to think that the exercise would keep us healthy. Of course this is not true, and you need to pay careful attention to your diet. Unfortunately, there are so many different ideas about the "right" diet it's difficult to know which is the best one for you.

What to eat

I think we are all aware of the importance of eating fresh produce, and getting the right combination of protein, grains and fruit and vegetables. Salads and raw vegetables are especially beneficial because they have not lost any nutrients due to cooking. Fish and chicken are better than red meat. Whey and soy products are a good substitute for animal protein. For the non-vegetarian eaters, I recommend having a 'vegetarian' day at least once a week. Your goal as a runner is to make sure you eat the best combination of foods to maintain a healthy body.

What not to eat

All the bad things you hear about fast foods are true! They shouldn't be part of your marathon training diet. The amount of saturated fat and low quality carbohydrates in fast foods will not help your training, and in excess will be detrimental to your overall health. When I line up for my morning coffee it's easy to spot the people who have had too many donuts for breakfast over the years! Frozen meals as well have lost a lot of their nutritional value due to the preparation process. Ever notice the sorry-looking broccoli you find in some of the 'dinner' plates? Finally those two standbys, coffee and alcohol, should only be consumed in moderation.

High carbs, low carbs, no carbs?

Complex carbohydrate intake from grains and pasta has long been recommended as the foundation of a running diet. This of course contradicts the dietary counsel of anyone trying to lose or maintain weight. Since these articles are focused on marathon training we have to look at your needs during the weeks leading up to the marathon. This could well be different from your normal diet. You definitely need to make sure you eat sufficient carbohydrates to help provide the energy you need on longer runs.

How much is enough?

When I'm not marathon training I prefer a lower carbohydrate based diet. You need to assess the intensity of your own training. If you are looking to run a faster marathon and have high weekly mileage you need to have a fairly high carb intake. My recommendations in terms of percentage of your calorie intake are as follows:

> **50 – 65 %** calories from complex carbohydrates

> **15 – 25%** calories from fat, unsaturated as much as possible

> **20 – 25%** calories from protein. Use the higher percentage if you are weight training

A typical dinner meal would provide the following calories and grams of carbohydrate, protein and fat.

Food Item	Calories	Carbs	Protein	Fat
Baked potato	200	51	5	0
Steamed broccoli	40	9	5	0
Cheese sauce	140	10	5	8
Carrots	50	16	2	0
5 oz. chicken skinless	200	0	25	6
Totals:	720	86	45	14
Approximate calorie %		55%	25%	20%

Of course this could vary a lot, depending on serving sizes. Usually though we often end up eating too much animal protein, which can be hard on your system if you overdo it.

The vegetarian runner
If you are in this group you already know the many health benefits of a vegetarian diet. When you are marathon training just make sure you are getting the carbohydrates you need, and also sufficient protein.

Carbo' loading vs. the Zone
When I am not doing marathon training I am a strong believer in the Zone diet also known as 40-30-30. I highly recommend you read one of Barry Sears' books about the zone. Briefly said, we should be getting our calories in the following proportions:

> ➢ 40% from carbohydrate
> ➢ 30% from protein
> ➢ 30% from fat (mostly unsaturated)

When I first picked up a copy of Sears' book the thing that grabbed my attention right away was the fact that the women's US Swim team had followed his regime, and scored an unprecedented success in the Olympics.

Another advantage of this diet in conjunction with endurance training is that your body will get some of its energy from fat on a regular basis. The body's switchover from burning calories from carbohydrates to fat is going to happen in the marathon anyway, and is one cause of "hitting the wall". On the zone diet your body gets more used to this, and will reduce the impact when you are actually running the marathon.

Alternate Fast Foods
Given the fast pace of modern life, we often don't have the time to prepare full meals. Here are a few alternates to the burger choice:

> ➤ **Chicken Caesar** makes a quick nutritious meal, add some carbohydrate.
> ➤ **Nuts** make great snacks and are packed with nutrients and vitamins
> ➤ **Bananas** make a simple snack and also contain potassium
> ➤ **Soups** like lentil soup have a lot of nutritional value and are also very filling!

Fruit and vegetables
Fruit and vegetables are full of vitamins and nutrients and are a great nutritional source that will contribute to your well-being. Since I started to watch my diet more carefully, and increased my intake of these foods I have seen many benefits. I have more energy and vitality; I don't get that afternoon tired feeling, and generally feel more positive about things.

Juicing
We bought a juicing machine several years ago, and I am convinced this is a great way to get all the benefits from vegetables, without having to eat huge servings. We enjoy a carrot and apple juice combination most mornings. Since the vegetables are juiced raw, you don't lose nutrients either. If you are in a hurry this is also a quick complement to a light meal. There are many books available on this topic if you are interested.

Water

We've all heard of the 8 glasses a day rule, but how many of us actually do it? The benefits of drinking lots of water are well known. Being properly hydrated will replenish the fluid lost through sweating and help you run faster.

> ➤ You should make a conscious effort to drink more water, especially as you approach the marathon race date.

Vitamin supplements

If you ate a good diet all the time you probably wouldn't need any supplements like vitamin "C" or "E". My take on this is that some supplements can be very beneficial and are worth the cost. I usually take vitamins B, C and E about four times a week. For men, Saw Palmetto extract is supposed to help guard against prostate problems. For those of us over 50, calcium supplements in moderation are good for guarding against osteoporosis.

Fish Oil

Remember your grandmother telling you to take your teaspoonful of cod liver oil. Well there are plenty of studies showing the benefits of a regular intake of fish oil. These include:

> ➤ Helping your oxygen uptake
> ➤ Fat burning
> ➤ Helping the body's joints to function better.

You can get these in capsule form for easy ingestion.

Benefits of a 'good' diet

We all have different opinions about what to eat, so ultimately it's your choice! I believe following basic principles like...

➢ Balanced proportions of carbohydrate, protein, fat
➢ Moderate calorific intake
➢ Plenty of fresh fruit and vegetables
➢ Moderate alcohol and coffee consumption
➢ Less sweets, and 'junk' food

...will make you feel better, and will help to improve your running.

Debbie's Footnotes:

Over the past ten years or so, Mike and I have tried various diet programs and have settled on what we found worked best for us. Experimenting while gaining knowledge and tuning into our own feelings of wellness is how we came to follow the Zone diet by Dr. Barry Sears. His program suited our need for balanced foods and gave us a better understanding of how the body works. You may already be on a diet program that is working for you. Before making any major diet or exercise changes be sure to consult your physician.

During marathon training it's a challenge not to give in to eating quick meals at fast food outlets. Healthy meals usually take longer to prepare and as you get into the longer training runs you have less time. I find planning ahead and doing some meal preparation in advance can help.

8: The Weekly Long Run

"Mental will is a muscle that needs exercise, like the muscles of the body." —Lynn Jennings[4]

---

[4] A pioneer of women's running, she was an Olympic medalist in the 10,000 meters in Barcelona in 1992. She broke several American records at the 3K, 5K and 10K distances.

The weekly long run is the cornerstone of your marathon training...

By gradually building up the distance during your training, you will be able to manage the 26.2 miles on race day. Since it is so important to the success of your training I am devoting a full chapter to this topic.

Purpose of the long run

The purpose of the long run is to build up strength and endurance and to get your body used to continuous exercise over an extended time. That's all -you don't need to run at your intended marathon pace, (or faster!), this can be counterproductive and will increase the risk of injury.

Approach with care!

Because you don't get a whole lot of rest days in a typical week's training the long run often feels hard. I recall struggling through a 14 miler and thinking how am I ever going to do another 12 in the marathon, and at a faster pace! (Don't worry though; it all seems to come together by the time marathon day arrives). The long runs put a lot of stress on your body, and can be a primary cause of injuries.

➔ Don't take your long run for granted – approach it like you would a race. If you're not feeling on form my advice is to postpone the long run to another day.

The build up

➔ One of the most common mistakes marathoners make is to increase their weekly long run distance too quickly.

The problem is not that your body can't handle it, - it's the time needed afterwards for recovery. I'm sure all of us have over-done the long run at some time, and then had to nurse sore legs back into the training routine. The goal here is to plan a gradual build up from say 6 or 7 miles at the start of training to 20 miles three weeks before the marathon. Over a sixteen week training period this would be an average weekly increase of a little under a mile.

Rest days around the long run
The hard day/easy day training concept definitely applies to the long run day.

> The difficult thing about marathon training is that in order to meet the weekly mileage goals you have to run most days. Your body does not really get enough time to recover from the long run.

Make sure you have an easy day, or a day off, the day before and the day after your long run. Your legs will be grateful!

Carbo' load?
As your long runs increase in distance you definitely need to carbo' load one to two days before the run. As your weekly distances increase, you should be eating plenty of quality complex carbohydrates like whole wheat grains and cereals. The traditional pasta dish the day before will help you get through the distance.

What pace to run?
You should do this run at a slower, more comfortable pace, always slower than your intended marathon pace. This is known as Long Slow Distance training – LSD. The aim is to get your body used to continuous

exercise for longer and longer periods. You can run at your marathon pace during shorter runs.

As indicated earlier, the goal is to build up your endurance gradually, not to simulate the actual race!

I normally do my long run at 30 – 60 seconds per mile slower than my marathon pace. This is important when you reach the 15 mile plus level. Some people prefer to do the long run based on time rather than distance.

Typical course
The long run is a good opportunity to run a varied course if possible. Many marathons include at least one significant hill, so try and include one in your run if possible. It's better to train on more challenging terrain than the marathon if you can, even if it's just for the psychological advantage of knowing you can do it. Since the key to successful training is 'moderation', don't overdo the hill work though, unless you are used to it.

Walking breaks
I have been a fan of walking breaks ever since I started to walk for 2 – 3 minutes during longer runs. One of the big benefits I have noticed is not feeling so sore the next day. In hot weather, taking the occasional walking break will allow your body to cool off as well.

Hydration
It is important to drink plenty of water during your long runs.

➜ If you start to get that dry parched feeling in your throat, its too late – you are already de-hydrated.

Be proactive and plan your long run route with plenty of water stops along the way. You won't be able to carry sufficient water in a bottle for a 20 mile run.

Energy gels
Lots of people I know use energy gels during their long runs. I've tried them but haven't noticed a whole lot of difference in my energy level. Reminds me of taking cold medicine – you don't feel much better but you might have felt worse without them! If they work for you however, you should take them while training so your body is accustomed when it comes to the marathon.

Weather

> ➢ The weather is a big factor on marathon day; so don't put off your long run if the weather is not the best.

I'm not advocating you run whatever the conditions - that could be dangerous when it's too hot or too cold. However you should go whenever possible just to help you face reality if the weather turns bad for the marathon. Just make sure you take the conditions into account. Dress warmly in layers if it's cold, take breaks if it's hot and humid. Train indoors if it's icy!

Recovery from the long run
You will benefit more from the long run if your body has time to recover. You should have an easy training day or a day off following the long run. If you have had a harder run, and are still feeling sore, extend the easy recovery days. Your body will be grateful and you will end up stronger!

This is when you need to follow the 'listen to your body' advice and adjust your training schedule as necessary.

Debbie's Footnotes:

 The long runs in marathon training are often approached with mixed feelings. Whether you anxiously anticipate them or dread them depends a lot on the days just before your long run. I've mostly enjoyed them because the gradual increase in mileage helps to give me a real sense of progress in my training.

Sometimes the daily tasks of living can overshadow your training goals and a day missed in your training runs can make the long run a dreaded event. Maybe it's been a stressful and tiring week of work or unexpected activities and the time for your daily run has been sabotaged. It happens to most of us once in awhile, but we just have to get back on the training wagon and keep focused.

I've found that when unexpected disruptions occur and the long run day is here, then it's best to go anyway. If I'm feeling tired then I just run slower and take a few walking breaks. The important thing is to do the long run whether it's your best day or not. Of course, if you're feeling just too tired to run at all, then it's best to put the long run off for a day or so, until you get back enough energy to sustain you through the run. You can always make up for the gap in your training schedule when you're feeling better.

Stretching is important after every run, but especially so following the long run. Sometimes adding a 5 or 10 minute walking break is a good way to cool down and end the run before doing your stretches. Stretching will help reduce the soreness and can help prevent injury from muscles tightening up and putting stress on the joints and bones.

The long run can often leave you with muscle soreness the day or two after the run. One method I like to use is soaking in a hot tub before going to bed and if my muscles are especially sore, I like to put in a little Epson salts. I find the salt baths very soothing and restorative. Besides, why not pamper yourself after that long run anyway.

Don't forget to celebrate your long runs. Mike and I always like to celebrate by going out for breakfast (brunch) following the run. It's a ritual we've enjoyed sharing over the years. It's not so important what you choose to do, but whatever you do following your long run, make it a celebration. After all, you deserve to feel good about the progress that you've made.

9: Keeping Focused

Half of this game is 90% mental! – Yogi Berra[5]

---

[5] Baseball player and manager in the '50s and '60s, well known for his famous quotes about sport and life in general.

As you get further into your training schedule sometimes it feels like it's getting harder not easier! Here are a few things you can do to help stay focused on your goal, and keep up the training intensity during those long weeks of training.

The two-hour goal

I set myself intermediate goals during training that give me something to look forward to long before the actual race itself. One of these is reaching the two-hour mark in my long run training. When you reach this mark -congratulate yourself on achieving a major milestone.

Other examples of goals you can set for yourself during training are things like the first 15 mile run, reaching 40 miles in a week, and of course completing the 20 mile long run.

Change your schedule

I sometimes change my long run day (which I normally do on Saturdays) just to add a little variety to the schedule. Another option is to skip the long run altogether and do longer runs during the week to make up some of the miles.

Run with your club

As you get into weeks 12 and beyond, you'll really appreciate running with your fellow club members, if you belong to a running club or a marathon training group. If not try and find someone you can run with from time to time, otherwise it gets awfully lonely out there!

Races

You should participate in some races during your marathon training. One or two 10K runs will help keep you 'sharp'. Just don't force too much though, or you may risk an injury. A half-marathon event about 4 or

5 weeks before the marathon is always a good warm up for the full distance. You should try and run this at your marathon pace or faster.

Maintain your focus.
As the training weeks go by it feels like the training has become the end goal, instead of the means to get there!

You need to remind yourself that running a marathon is a big deal! That's why you are going through all this training. I used to say (half joking):

The marathon isn't so hard; it's the training that kills you!

The key point here is to keep a positive mental attitude towards the whole thing. Be prepared to adjust your training if circumstances change.

Monitor your progress
This is where keeping a logbook really helps. As the training weeks go by it's easy to lose track of where you are in your schedule. It helps to look back over the previous weeks and see what you have accomplished and what you have missed out.

Tapering Off
Make sure you follow your schedule closely in the last two or three weeks before the marathon. You reduce you weekly mileage to allow your body time to recover from all of the training. This way you can 'peak' for the actual race. Avoid the temptation to cut back on the time allocated to tapering if you are behind schedule – see below.

Behind Schedule?

For one reason or another you may find you are not where you should be at this point in your training. Maybe you started late, or missed some time due to an injury. Whatever the reason, you haven't reached your scheduled weekly mileage goal or your long run goal and marathon date is approaching fast. What do you do?

The first thing is what <u>not</u> to do:

➜ Don't try and make major increases in your weekly mileage and long run too quickly. You will probably do more harm than good.

If you are only a week behind you can probably catch up easily. If you're two or thee weeks away however, it's time to make some tough decisions! Dropping out of the marathon is not an easy choice, especially if it's one of the big ones with limited entry, like New York. If you've missed a lot of training however, this might be the only option.

By far the best solution is to revise your finish time goal, and aim for a (much) easier marathon. This will include planned walking breaks during the race. Believe me, I have run a marathon on minimum training without changing anything, and suffered afterwards!

Debbie's Footnotes

 What makes the difference between marathon runners that make it to the start and finish lines and those that don't? When you start out on the training schedule, the goal of running the marathon seems so far away, but time passes quickly and before long you'll be looking back at the weeks and wonder how you're progressing. Whether you are off track or on with your fitness level and weekly mileage goals will largely depend on how well you have stayed focused on your goals. The secret to staying focused during the weeks of training is to look at your schedule before and after each week of training. Bringing the weekly goals to the front of your mind will strengthen your resolve to meet the end goal.

Reviewing your progress and seeing what you want to focus on that week will help identify the adjustments needed to make improvements in your training for the day of the race. For example, one week you may need to ease up on your intensity to increase your weekly long run distance. Or you may need to increase your intensity and get your fitness level up to accomplish the pace for your time goals? Do you need to focus on eating better to sustain the energy for the weekly training goals? Whatever your goals are, it's important to stay focused along the way.

10: Pre-Race Week

"Tough times don't last but tough people do." -A.C. Green[6]

---

[6] NBA player with a record of 1,192 consecutive games

This is a critical week in your program. The reduced mileage gives the body plenty of rest and recovery from all the training you've been doing. Here are some things you need to pay attention to during this final training week.

Rest and Relaxation

This is the 'order of the day'. You can ruin your race if you try to do too much during this week. Make sure you get plenty of sleep. I often don't sleep too well the night before, especially if I have traveled to the marathon, so I try and get a really good sleep two days prior to the race. Try to keep your stress level low too, by purposely avoiding the common 'stressors' in your life.

Running

You won't be running much during this week. I recommend two relaxed runs, about 7 and 4 days before the actual race. I also like to run an easy three miles the day before the race, just to keep the 'parts' moving. However this is probably more mental than anything else.

Here is a typical week:

Mon	Tue	Wed	Thu	Fri	Sat	Sun
5	0	4	0	0	3	26

Whatever you do, avoid the temptation (because you are feeling strong) to do a 'last' hard or long run before the marathon. You don't want to wreck all of that good training with a mistake in the final week.

Diet

> ➢ What you eat is very important as you approach the big event.

I have experimented with various dietary modifications during the week before (usually over-indulging in Carbo-loading foods!) and have come to the conclusion that it didn't help my performance, and may even have hindered. My recommendation is to stick with what you have been doing during training.

If you have read the chapter on eating, then you know that I really like the Zone diet as one that is excellent for athletes. I follow this throughout the week, with extra carbohydrates thrown in. I go with the pasta dinner the night before, more out of tradition than anything. I have had no ill effects from doing this, but you need to follow your own preferences here.

➔ Your training is the best time to try out some variations in your food intake to see how things go without taking a huge risk.

Hydration

> ➢ You also need to drink plenty of water. Not just the day before – the whole week.

This is partly based on my belief that you shouldn't do anything too much out of the ordinary (i.e. consuming a whole lot more liquids than normal) the day before a marathon. A good intake (10 to 12 glasses) of water the day before will help make sure you are well hydrated at race time.

The Mental Aspect
Every little ache and pain seems to be magnified by a factor of 10 in the pre-race week. If you are a worrier, then you are going to spend a lot of time concerned about your health and readiness for the race. If you have made it this far into the training I say "Don't

Worry". I have gone to the start line many times concerned about aches that weren't there a week ago! But as soon as the race got started, and I warmed up, I totally forgot about any residual pains.

It helps to visualize the race in your mind. If you have had a chance to go over the course by car previously, this will be a tremendous help when you are actually running the race.

Not that it makes it any shorter, but it's good to know what's coming up, where the halfway point is, etc.

The day before the race

> To sum it up in three words – Take it Easy! Don't spend hours on your feet sightseeing or browsing the race Expo. Sure you can do some of this, but you need to have plenty of R & R.
> Try an easy (slower than your marathon pace) 3 mile run the morning before. It certainly has helped me to keep loosened up for the race on the following day.
> Don't over-eat, and stick with the foods your body can handle. I normally have a salad for lunch and then the pre-race pasta supper in the early evening. Don't have much alcohol either, one beer or a glass of wine is enough.
> Get your gear ready for the next day (don't forget the sun block and Vaseline). You don't want to be rushing around looking for your favorite pair of socks just before it's time to leave.
> Go to bed early, so you won't have a hard time getting up the next day.

Debbie's Footnotes:

 All weeks of training I suppose can be seen as pre-race weeks, but the final week before the big event is probably the most important of all. This final week is the best of all too. Finally, after all those preceding weeks of training you can now 'take it easy' as you should. You've got the hard part of the training behind you and the race is all that is left. Of course, it's the hardest of all, but during the pre-race week the focus is more on what not to do than what to do. The main goal of this week is to make the race experience more enjoyable (less hurtful).

There are definite ways to conserve your energy for race day. I like to do the things that I've not taken time to do during the training weeks, like go for leisurely walks with my camera and take photos of the things I've enjoyed seeing along my running routes. Also it's a time to sit back and put your feet up, something that you've probably not done much of during the training. I like to catch up on my reading and finish the book that has been sitting on my nightstand for weeks because I've been too tired to read much at the end of the day.

 Since the race is just a few days away, it's a good time to read up on the marathon event and get familiar with the course and city as well as the activities scheduled before and after the event. Reading articles on running keeps me hyped for the race day and keeps me focused on my marathon goal. During the pre race week one of the hardest things to do is to keep from going out for the usual runs. I sometimes get fidgety legs during the pre race week because they're use to being exercised. This week is about <u>not</u> running more than it is about running, so when that happens I just take an aspirin or that pampered bath to calm the fidgets.

Keep a bottle of water with you at all times wherever you go and drink lots of water. On race day you'll be glad you did. Staying positive about your ability to complete the marathon is important. Remember you are ready, you've done the training and the race day is the chance for you to prove you are a marathon runner. Stay calm and be confident. You'll sleep better and do better in the marathon.

11: Marathon Day Strategies

"Believe in yourself, know yourself, deny yourself, and be humble." - John Treacy's[7] four principles of training prior to Los Angeles

[7] Famous Irish runner, Olympic Marathon Silver medal, 1984 and World Cross-Country champion, 1979, 1980

Are you ready? Of course you are – you just spent 16 weeks or more training for this day!

Pre-race Preparation

➢ **Get up early,** so you have plenty of time to get ready before setting out.

➢ **Wear suitable clothing**. Sometimes it's difficult to know what to wear, especially since many marathons take place in the changeable seasons of Spring and Fall. Listen to the weather forecast (and hope they're right!), and dress accordingly. When I'm not sure I usually go with the lighter option such as a singlet versus T-shirt.

➢ **Warm-up clothes are necessary** if it's a cold morning. You don't want to get too cold waiting for the race to start. Anything from garbage bags to old T-shirts or sweatshirts will do. I like the T-shirt/sweatshirt option because you can actually start the race, and get rid of it later at an aid station.

➢ **Creams.** Avoid a burn by putting on plenty of sun block with a high SPF. You will be out there for several hours, and could get a nasty burn on a warm sunny day. If you are subject to chafing (and even if you are not) it's a good idea to put some Vaseline on the tender spots like the under-arm and groin.

➢ **Drink more water.** You're probably sick of drinking water by now; but you should drink a glass or so before heading out to the start line.

> ➤ **Have a light breakfast.** I don't recommend you skip breakfast. If you have something light such as toast and a banana you shouldn't suffer any adverse effects. During my training I always have a light breakfast before my weekly long runs so my body is used to the routine.
>
> ➤ **Pre-race warm up -** Keep moving when you get to the starting area. It's OK to rest, but you should do a light warm-up such as an easy jog or brisk walk for 5 minutes or so, just before the race. Of course this is much harder to do at the mega-marathons like New York and Chicago with all the crowds.

Strategy

A race strategy will help you run the best marathon you can. There are many things that can affect you during this long event. If you have thought about them previously then you should be prepared to adjust during the run and complete a successful marathon.

> ➜ What is a 'Successful Marathon'? For me, a successful marathon is one in which I was able to finish without hitting the wall and without too much pain. If I come close to my target time so much the better.

Key factors that will affect your performance during the race are:

> ➤ Your target time and pace
> ➤ Your conditioning and fitness level
> ➤ The weather
> ➤ Liquid intake
> ➤ The marathon course

The effect of each of these on your final result is discussed in detail below.

Your target time and pace

> I believe an over-optimistic target time and race pace is the primary cause of marathoners running into problems such as leg cramps, hitting the wall and running out of energy well before the end of the race.

One of the most important things you can do at the start of the race is take into account the main factors that can affect your performance *and adjust your initial pace accordingly.*
"But if I go slower at the beginning" you say, "I'll never meet my goal". Wrong!

> The common belief that you will slow down in the second half is only true because you went out too fast in the first half!

I know because I've done it both ways! So, if it's a warm day, or a challenging course take those first few miles easy (30 seconds to one minute slower than your "intended" pace), and see how things work out. Don't expect to run the complete race at exactly the same pace – it just doesn't happen that way.

Your conditioning and fitness level

If you haven't done enough training then you are probably going to have a tough time, unless you take it really easy. On the other hand if you have done too much hard training you could also get tired long before mile 26. This is difficult to judge at the start of a race, but you should look back over your training anyway. Did you run a 20 miler less than three weeks prior to the marathon for example?

Have you caught a cold recently? I normally monitor my pulse rate on a regular basis during training. If this is elevated on race day, it's a sign that your body might be fighting an infection.

➜ Remember if you are not feeling 100% fit, you should modify your target finish time.

The weather
The weather can have a huge impact on your race. It can be too hot, too cold, too windy, too everything! Personally, when I am training I try to go out in adverse conditions just in case that's the way marathon day turns out.
I've had the most difficulty when the weather has been warmer than expected. (Remembering a Boston marathon one year in a sunny 70^0 plus temperature).

> ➢ It is most important that you start out slower to compensate for adverse weather until you body has adjusted to the conditions. Then you can gradually pick up the pace.

If you are running into a headwind, you will be using more energy than normal, and will tire too soon if you keep pushing the pace early on.

Liquid Intake
Your body needs to be kept hydrated during the race. Most marathon courses are well equipped with water stops throughout the race, so there is no excuse for not taking enough liquid. But I've done exactly that. I ran past the first few water stops figuring I didn't need it. I realize now, if you wait until you are thirsty, then it's probably too late!

→ Make sure you stop for water frequently, right from the start of the race.

The Marathon Course

It helps a lot if you are familiar with the marathon course, either because you have run it before or you have driven it. Many marathons boast of a 'flat' course but when you're at mile 18 even a slight incline can feel like a mountain if you are struggling. If the course is known for having some challenging spots like Heartbreak Hill at Boston, my advice is to ease up before you get there so you have some energy in reserve.

Debbie's Footnotes

 All that training and marathon day is finally here. You're up early and, hopefully slept well, so you're rested and ready for those last minute details of race day morning.   You look out the window and see what the weather looks like and check the local temperature. Of course, this is the twentieth time you've checked the weather forecast over the past few days. Since you packed for all types of weather, now it's time to choose the best match for the conditions of the day.

What about breakfast, to have or not to have, that is the question. As Mike said, we typically eat a light breakfast on our long run days, so we do the same on race day. Be sure though if you eat anything to allow plenty of time before the race starts so your food can digest or you may get cramps during the race.

We always drink extra water the morning of the race and what about bathroom breaks? Always be sure to use the bathroom a couple of times before the race starts. I once had to go after the start of the race and went into the bushes because there was no port-a-potty available.

We usually do a pre-course check out and try and talk with someone who has ran to course in the past. This allows us to be more prepared for the mental and physical challenges of each course. If the course is hilly we pace ourselves accordingly. Also, try and do some kind of warm up exercise before the race starts, but I prefer not to run much. I find that completing the 26.2 miles is enough for my energy stores. It's difficult sometimes to keep warm while waiting for a race to start, so I just keep moving or running in place until the gun goes off. I think it is best to use the first two or three miles as a warm up.

My strategy during the race is simply to make it to the finish line and hopefully in about four hours time. My best finish time was the first marathon probably because I went out more cautiously since I didn't know what to expect. My second and third marathon finish time was 20 minutes longer than the first, which I didn't expect. It's difficult to know what you will feel like in those last tough miles. The more marathons you run the more experience you will have in knowing what strategies work for you during the race.

12: The Race

"If you want to win something, run 100 meters. If you want to experience something, run a marathon". - Emil Zatopek[8]

---

[8] One of the greatest runners of the 20th Century, Emil Zatopek won the 5,000, the 10,000 and the marathon at the 1952 Olympic Games in Helsinki.

26 miles is a long way, and quite intimidating especially if it's your first marathon. This 'virtual' account tries to capture some of the things you will be thinking and feeling as you make your way over the 26.2 mile course.

Race day has finally arrived, and after several months of training you are anxious to get going. You wake up early, even though it was a bit of a restless night. After a cup of coffee and a slice of toast you get ready and head for the starting area. It's a cool morning and as you look around at the other runners you notice a wide assortment of gear. From shorts & singlets to long pants and sweatshirts. Some folks are wearing a plastic bag over their running clothes to ward off the early morning chill.

Finally the starting ceremony is over, and everyone shuffles forward. The pace is slow at first as the front of the pack gradually gets going. With the race chip on your shoe however, you are assured of a correct time once you reach the actual start line.

As the first mile gets underway you feel quite good, but deliberately keep the pace a little slower than your intended average pace. You pass mile one about 30 seconds over which is OK – there is plenty of time to make that up. Your goal is to run the second half faster than the first, and finish as comfortably as possible.

You pass a group of people carrying a balloon with '4½ HOURS' written on it, - 50 minutes over your own target time. "I hope I don't see them again," you think! The sun has risen higher and the temperature is climbing. You're glad you opted for shorts and singlet.

The second water stop appears and you slow down for
a quick drink even though you are not thirsty.

You settle into a steady pace and soon the 3-mile
mark comes up. You check your watch and see you
are about 1 minute over your average pace time. You
drove over the course yesterday, and remember there
is a hill just after the 3-mile mark. Here it is – and it
feels a little steeper than it did in the car. Longer too!

"It's getting warm already" you say to the guy running
next to you.

"Maybe it'll rain"! He replies.

You both laugh since it's a clear blue sky above. You
chat for a while and the next few miles go by easily.
Before you know it, the 6-mile mark comes up. Wow –
only 20 (.2) miles left, you think.

Your companion drops back a little as you continue at
your pace. You are still about one minute slower than
your pace time at the 6-mile mark. You notice a lot of
people chatting to each other as they run. At this
stage of the race everyone is still feeling good!
Spectators along the route clap and shout words of
encouragement as you go by. It all helps!

The race route wanders through an old neighborhood
full of large houses and treed lawns. The shade is
welcome. The miles don't seem to go by quite as
quickly as they did earlier. You're looking for the 10-
mile mark – there's a water stop ahead and the 10-
mile point is just past that. You check your time – still
about a minute over. Oh well, you think, that's OK.

Your next goal is the halfway mark. You think about all
the training you have done, so getting to the half
should be no problem. It seems to be taking a long
time to get there however. Finally you see the halfway
water stop. You walk through, enjoying the water and

the break from running. At least the miles go down from here on, 13, 10, 6...
You are beginning to feel the effect of the miles, but it's not too bad so far.

You talk to some of your fellow runners as you go along. Their previous marathon experiences are interesting to hear. 16 miles!! You'd been so busy talking you missed the 15 mile mark. You now feel you can finish the race without too many problems. You decide to pick up the pace a little to try and get back to your target time. You pull away from the group as you go up a slight incline.

Near mile 18 things are starting to get a little tough. You go up a short but steep hill, and feel like walking. Your energy seems to be getting low. At the next water stop you take some Gatorade instead of water. The sugar tastes good! You take a brief walk break and concentrate on getting to the 20 mile mark. Another runner pulls alongside, and you run together without saying much beyond 'Hi'. At last the 20-mile mark comes up.

To your surprise, you have made up the minute you were behind, and are actually a little under your target time. Encouraged by this you press on. You come to an incline that feels way steeper than it really is. Your companion pulls away as you struggle a little. Then you come to a downhill stretch and are able to lengthen your stride as you go down. It feels good after that last hill. Mile 21 comes up – the miles are definitely going slower at this point. Another shot of Gatorade and you keep on.

Only 5 more miles you think, and settle back into a comfortable pace. The weak spot you hit back at miles 18 and 19 seems to have passed. You keep going and reach mile 23, the end of the race definitely feels close. You keep to your pace, and try to think about other things than your weary legs.

"Looking good – only 2 more miles" you hear. You are feeling tired now but being so close you keep running. You catch up with the person you were running with a little earlier. You exchange a few words and run on together. At mile 25 your fellow runner takes off – you don't even try to keep up. Your focus is on getting through the last mile. The temperature is much warmer now and you are feeling thirsty even though you have taken a drink at most of the water stops.

Mile 26!! You made it you say to yourself, and start to run a little quicker. The last 0.2 miles seems long though, finally you see the finish banner up ahead. Lots of people are along the route. "Good run" they say. Your name is called over the PA system as you approach the finish line. You notice the time – 1 minute faster than your goal. You have run the second half faster than the first one!

In the finish chute you meet up with your last companion. "Great run', you say to each other. It feels really good to have completed the race without seriously 'hitting the wall'. You pick up your medal and head off to enjoy some of the fresh fruit in the finish area. As you relax, you're already thinking about the next marathon, and maybe cutting a few minutes off the time...

Debbie's Footnotes

 I don't like the stress of competition, so I prefer to think of a marathon (or any race for that matter) more as a run than a race. People get hyped up before the race and for some this works well, but if you're not comfortable with competition, just relax and approach the race as a 26-mile long run.

OK, you're at the starting line and people are looking each other over…. checking out the competition! You're anxious to get started. The gun fires and you're off. Remember rule #1 - *start out slow*. Maybe you're caught up in the excitement and think; maybe I can go out a bit faster. DON'T! If you do, you'll regret it 'big time' later on. Ease into the run just like you did on those long training runs and you'll do better in your finish time.

Maintaining energy levels during the marathon is vital. After the first couple of miles my muscles are warmed up and I get into a rhythm and do fine until about mile 10 or 12 depending on the course and the temperature. I carry some dextrose tablets or lifesavers with me and start to take them about this time. I find they help keep my glucose levels from getting too low. Also, try and take short walking breaks at the water stops. Don't walk too long though or your muscles may relax too much and start to stiffen up. A 30 second walk during the water stops allows time to take enough water to hydrate you and will help keep you running later instead of walking the last tough miles.

Try not to concentrate too much on the discomforts during the race, rather, keep your mind focused on enjoying the participation and finishing the race. The sense of accomplishment that you'll feel with completing a marathon is what makes it all worthwhile.

13: Marathon Recovery

"A good beginning makes a good ending" - English proverb

Running a marathon takes its toll on you, both physically and mentally. How well you recover depends on your activity level and attitude during the weeks following the race.

Things to do after the race

Although you probably don't feel like it – you should walk around the finish area for fifteen minutes or so. Do some stretching as well to help your muscles gradually relax. Eating some of the post race snacks like bananas and apples is beneficial. Make sure to drink plenty of water and a sports drink like Gatorade.

I would often take a warm bath after I returned home, just to relax. However many experts say this can aggravate sore muscles. So if you do want to take a bath, make sure the water is not too hot.

If you have any sore muscles, try an ice pack for a few minutes. An anti-inflammatory like Ibuprofen may help. Treat blisters and chafes right away to avoid any infection that could occur.

You can look forward to a good dinner that evening with plenty of carbohydrates. My personal preference is to add some good quality protein like lean steak or chicken breast.

Resuming running

How soon after your marathon should you start running?

This is another of these frequently asked questions with opposing answers. Some people swear that you shouldn't run for at least a week. Others say run after a few days to clear out the lactic acid build-up in the calf muscles.

Here is my take on this question. Both answers are correct, and it depends on whether you had a hard marathon or not. If you hit the wall (i.e. you encountered a sudden dramatic drop in your energy level, and your legs felt like lead.), were forced to walk, and generally limped in the last six miles or so then you had a hard race. My recommendation is take it easy and do some walking instead of running.

On the other hand if you had a relatively comfortable marathon and came in close to your intended time without too much pain and suffering then you will probably benefit from running three easy miles about three days after the race. Everybody is different though; so don't push it if your body starts to complain after the first few steps!

Muscle soreness can actually get worse two or three days after the marathon.

You definitely need to take it easy if you feel this happening. After my first marathon, I couldn't walk downstairs comfortably for almost a week! Running during this time was out of the question.

The Recovery Period

How long does it take to recover completely from the marathon?

Again, the answer depends on the difficulties you encountered during the race. A standard rule-of thumb is one day per mile, or twenty-six days!

I have known people who run another marathon within two weeks. (Eeks!!) This is definitely <u>not</u> recommended.

When you resume regular running after a week or two, expect to be tired, even on short runs. After about five miles I usually feel like I've had enough. This can persist for a couple of weeks and the best thing is to simply listen to what your body is trying to tell you. Take it easy!

Once you get through this recovery period you will be feeling quite strong again, and ready for new challenges.

Tapering in Reverse

Just as you tapered off with decreasing weekly mileage in the weeks just prior to the marathon you need to do the opposite after the race. Here is a typical post race schedule:

Week 1:

Mon	Tue	Wed	Thu	Fri	Sat	Sun
0	0	Walk	3	0	Walk	4

Week 2:

Mon	Tue	Wed	Thu	Fri	Sat	Sun
0	4	Walk	0	5	0	6

➔ I have found walking breaks during my recovery runs have been extremely beneficial.

I believe that the lower impact from walking relieves the stress on your muscle tissue, but you still get the benefit of the increased blood flow from the exercise.

➔ You should also avoid running hills during the recovery period.

If you have access to off-road trails, your legs will appreciate the softer surface.

Cross training

Another great way to help you recover is cross training. Swimming and cycling are good examples of low impact sports that provide you with the benefits of aerobic exercise without the pounding.

Don't cross train in addition to your running though. These are good substitutes during the recovery. I find it helps to maintain one of the cross training activities even after I have fully recovered.

Staying Healthy

Running the marathon will weaken your immune system, making you more vulnerable to catching colds or flu'. It can take three or four days before your immune system has recuperated. During this time you need to reduce stress, take vitamin supplements and eat healthy.

Foods to Eat

Your diet is important during the recovery period. You need balanced amounts of carbohydrates and protein, with some (unsaturated) fat. Fresh fruit and vegetables will provide your body with lots of nutrients and vitamins. Nuts and seeds make healthy snacks.

Although this will not suit everyone's palate, you will benefit from eating raw vegetables and salads. Carrots, cauliflower and broccoli are very good for you and easy to eat. If you have a juicing machine you should try some vegetable and apple combination juices. This will give your immune system a 'boost'.

Mental Recovery

After weeks of training and focusing on the race, it's finally over. Now what?

After completing the marathon, many people experience a feeling of depression and lack of interest in resuming running. "I'm too tired" is a frequent rationale for not getting back into the regular routine.

This can be related to your marathon performance. If you met or exceeded your expectations and had a good race and easy recovery, you are less likely to feel this way. Whatever the case, it helps to recognize the symptoms and take action to minimize the problem.

> ➢ A cross training activity can help because it's different from running and that puts you in another mindset.

Talking about your experience with family and friends is also good. Don't forget, the fact that you crossed the finish line puts you in a special 'club' of marathon finishers. This is a major accomplishment and you need to enjoy the moment.

A running club is anther great way to overcome the post-marathon blues. It's interesting to learn about the other runners' marathon experiences, and their plans for the next one.

> ➢ Before you know it you'll be caught up in the enthusiasm (and yes, bravado!) and you'll be planning on improving your time in your next marathon attempt.

Debbie's Footnotes.

Ahhh...the race is over, but the recovery is just beginning. What is recovery? Just like the marathon it can be quite an experience. There are a lot of variables to whether you have an easy or hard recovery process. Much depends on how well you did in the marathon training, your fitness level and course conditions on race day. I've found the longer my run time the longer the recovery time. I've had post marathon runs that felt comfortable and ones that hurt and I ended up walking for days after.

What matters most in recovery is that you keep active, doing whatever feels good just as long as you keep moving and exercising to maintain the aerobic benefits and keep the blood flowing through your veins.

During the first two, three and even fourth weeks following a marathon it's OK to just exercise...not train...that was before.... now you are just exercising for the joy and benefit of it. This can help offset the post marathon 'blues' that some people experience. Sure there's no big goal to focus on, but fully embracing the recovery is well worth the time and patience. Yes, if you do a good recovery program you'll be back out on the course again before long and getting ready for the next big race. Just remember though that recovery means slow down, recuperate and give your body, mind and spirit time to rejuvenate.
Recovery is different for everyone and will depend a lot on you race experience, fitness level, lifestyle and age.

14. Last thoughts...

"Perseverance is not a long race; it is many short races, one after another" - Walter Elliott[9]

---

[9] Scottish writer and politician

We hope you enjoyed reading Marathon Training Tips and that it will help you to run a better marathon. If you have any comments on the book or would like to tell us how your marathon went, please email us at:

feedback@personallogs.com

We look forward to hearing from you!

As Mike mentioned in the preface the main goal of this book is to focus on marathon training. There are many resources available both in book form and on the Web that deal in depth with the topics covered here. Recovering from an injury is a good example. Try typing in "shin splints" on Google search and you'll end up with pages of links to sites about this common problem. Of course you need to take time to check out the sites and find which ones seem relevant to you. There is also lots of advice available about choosing the right running shoe for you.

We have also tried throughout the book to make it clear that 'one size does not fit all' and every marathoner is different. If you find you are doing some things differently from what we proposed - as long as they work for you - don't worry. (We do advise you to try to follow the key points and 'golden rules' however).

In the final analysis, running a marathon is a major undertaking and once you cross the finish line you have proved that you can accomplish what your mind dictates.

Appendix A: Pacing Chart

Pace per mile		5K	10K	15K	20K	1/2 Marathon	Marathon	Miles per Hour
Mins	Secs	h:mm:ss	h:mm:ss	h:mm:ss	h:mm:ss	h:mm:ss	h:mm:ss	mph
4	30	0:13:57	0:27:54	0:41:51	0:55:48	0:58:57	1:57:54	13.33
5	00	0:15:30	0:31:00	0:46:30	1:02:00	1:05:30	2:11:00	12.00
5	30	0:17:03	0:34:06	0:51:09	1:08:12	1:12:03	2:24:06	10.91
6	00	0:18:36	0:37:12	0:55:48	1:14:24	1:18:36	2:37:12	10.00
6	30	0:20:09	0:40:18	1:00:27	1:20:36	1:25:09	2:50:18	9.23
7	00	0:21:42	0:43:24	1:05:06	1:26:48	1:31:42	3:03:24	8.57
7	30	0:22:56	0:45:53	1:08:49	1:31:46	1:36:56	3:13:53	8.11
8	00	0:24:48	0:49:36	1:14:24	1:39:12	1:44:48	3:29:36	7.50
8	30	0:26:21	0:52:42	1:19:03	1:45:24	1:51:21	3:42:42	7.06
9	00	0:27:54	0:55:48	1:23:42	1:51:36	1:57:54	3:55:48	6.67
9	30	0:29:27	0:58:54	1:28:21	1:57:48	2:04:27	4:08:54	6.32
10	00	0:31:00	1:02:00	1:33:00	2:04:00	2:11:00	4:22:00	6.00
10	30	0:32:33	1:05:06	1:37:39	2:10:12	2:17:33	4:35:06	5.71
11	00	0:34:06	1:08:12	1:42:18	2:16:24	2:24:06	4:48:12	5.45
11	30	0:35:39	1:11:18	1:46:57	2:22:36	2:30:39	5:01:18	5.22
12	00	0:37:12	1:14:24	1:51:36	2:28:48	2:37:12	5:14:24	5.00

Download the Excel version of this pacing chart from our website:
www.personallogs.com/PacingChart.php

Appendix B: More Resources

Here are some additional resources you might want to check out to help improve your marathon running or your running in general. Most of these are websites you can access quickly for relevant information.

Marathon Training:

Marathon Guide: This online magazine contains a lot of useful articles about the marathon. They also maintain a 'Races' page that contains a comprehensive list of marathon races in the US and Canada.

www.marathonguide.com

Marathon & Beyond is a magazine tailored specifically for marathoners and ultra runners. Their website is:

www.marathonandbeyond.com

Running:

Personal Logs: This is our website where we feature personalized sports logs for running, cycling, triathlon and walking. We also maintain a page for marathon training and general running. You can download an interactive **Pace Chart** and the **training schedules** found in this book. We are also working on more running related information you can download in the near future.

www.personallogs.com

Dr. Sheehan was a long time runner who wrote many interesting articles and books about running. His philosophical approach to the sport is both inspiring and informative. This website is maintained by his children.

www.georgesheehan.com

Health & Diet:

Doctor Barry Sears' website about the Zone diet. This has a wealth of information, including a list of Dr. Sears' books, dealing with the Zone diet and its benefits.

www.drsears.com

Sports Injury Clinic: This website has some good information on running related injuries and how to avoid them. They also discuss treatment if you do suffer from an injury.

www.sportsinjuryclinic.net

Your Race Results

Use these pages to record all your race results in one handy location.

Date	Race Name / Location	Dist.	Your Time	Category Placing	Overall Placing
Comments:					
Comments:					
Comments:					
Comments:					
Comments:					
Comments:					
Comments:					
Comments:					

Your Race Results

Date	Race Name / Location	Dist.	Your Time	Category Placing	Overall Placing
Comments:					
Comments:					
Comments:					
Comments:					
Comments:					
Comments:					
Comments:					
Comments:					

Notes

Use this page to record any additional information you might want to refer back to in the future.

.

CPSIA information can be obtained at www.ICGtesting.com
Printed in the USA
LVOW032039301111

257181LV00005B/253/A